THE BEAR
WHO HAD NO PLACE
TO GO

by James Stevenson

HARPER & ROW, PUBLISHERS
New York, Evanston, San Francisco, London

THE BEAR WHO HAD NO PLACE TO GO

Copyright © 1972 by James Stevenson

All rights reserved. Printed in the United States of America. No part of this book may be used or reproduced in any manner whatsoever without written permission except in the case of brief quotations embodied in critical articles and reviews. For information address Harper & Row, Publishers, Inc., 10 East 53rd Street, New York, N.Y. 10022. Published simultaneously in Canada by Fitzhenry & Whiteside Limited, Toronto.

Library of Congress Catalog Card Number: 70-186775
Trade Standard Book Number: 06-025780-6
Harpercrest Standard Book Number: 06-025781-4

Format by Kohar Alexanian

CHAPTERS

Without a Job   5

On the Road   14

The Woods   26

Without a Job

Ralph was a bear who rode a bicycle in the circus. When the circus band played, Ralph went around and around the ring on his bike.

Everybody loved to see Ralph ride, especially when he did "no hands." The crowd clapped and cheered. Ralph was very proud.

Ralph liked almost everything about the circus. But after the last show, the crowds went home, and the other animals were put into their cages. Ralph would watch the roustabouts take down the big tent in the moonlight, and he would feel all alone.

Late at night he would ride on the special circus train to the next town. And before he went to sleep, Ralph would look at the country going by.

Then he would get into his striped pajamas, climb into his berth, listen to the wheels of the train clacking, and watch the stars until he fell asleep.

One day, Mr. Doll, who was the boss of the circus, said to Ralph, "I have bad news for you, kid. You have been a terrific bicycle-rider, but the circus needs a new act. I have hired a seal who can play 'Stars and Stripes Forever' on horns, and this seal is taking your place."

"Taking my place?" said Ralph.

"Yeah," said Mr. Doll. "We can't use you anymore. Sorry, Ralph."

Ralph couldn't believe it. The circus was the only life he knew.

"You can keep the bike, Ralph," said Mr. Doll. "Good luck."

That night, after the show was over, Ralph went around and said good-bye to all the circus people and animals.

For the last time he watched the roustabouts take down the tent and put everything on the train. Then, when the whole circus was aboard—except for Ralph—the whistle tooted, and Ralph watched the train go away without him.

After a while, Ralph put on his pajamas and tried to go to sleep, but it was hard to sleep without the sound of train wheels clacking. It was very quiet. It was too quiet, and too dark, and much too lonely.

When Ralph woke up it was morning. Nobody was around. He decided to get on his bike and find someplace where there were people, and things happening. He put his pajamas on the bicycle seat, and started off.

On the Road

Soon Ralph came to a big highway. There were lots of cars and trucks, and they were all going very fast. A sign said TO THE CITY. Everybody honked their horns at Ralph because he wasn't going fast enough, and a lot of people glared at him. Ralph pedaled faster.

When he finally got to the city, Ralph didn't know what to do. All the people were walking very fast. Nobody said hello. It was noisy and hot. Ralph sat down in the shade to think.

The people kept rushing by. It was like the crowd coming to the circus, but there were no children, and nobody was laughing.

Ralph decided to get out of the city and look for a small town. The highway went through a lot of places that were smoky and smelly. After a while, Ralph came to a small town that looked okay.

Ralph decided he would try to get a job. He went into a grocery store and told the man that he would like to deliver groceries on his bicycle.

"How could you carry them?" asked the man.

"I happen to be able to ride with no hands," said Ralph.

"Let's see," said the man.

Ralph picked up a box of groceries and got on his bike and started to ride.

"Not bad," said the man. "Take them to the yellow house at the end of the street."

Ralph was doing fine when suddenly an old circus poster caught his eye. He forgot where he was and what he was doing—all Ralph could think of was the circus. He could almost hear the band, and smell the popcorn, and then—

Ralph crashed into a policeman who was standing on the corner. The groceries went flying.

"I'm very sorry," said Ralph. "I was delivering these groceries."

The policeman stared at him.

Then the grocer ran up.

"Does this bear work for you?" asked the policeman.

"Not any more, Officer," said the grocer.

Ralph picked up the groceries and gave them to the man, and said he was sorry again. Then he got on his bike and rode out of town into the country.

Ralph was feeling very sad and lonely. Then it started to rain. As he came to the top of a hill, he saw a rat hitchhiking at the side of the road. The rat looked very wet.

Ralph stopped. "Want a lift?" he asked.

"Sure do," said the rat. "Thanks." He climbed onto the handlebars. "Where did you find the cool bike?" he asked.

"I used to be in the circus," said Ralph, starting to pedal.

"The *circus*?" said the rat. "Wow! It's a pleasure to meet a famous performer. My name's Frank."

"I'm Ralph," said Ralph.

"How come you left the circus?" said Frank. "Got tired of all the bright lights and excitement, I suppose?"

"No. I got replaced by a seal," said Ralph.

"A seal on a bicycle?" said Frank. "That's some act! Wow!"

"No. He played horns," said Ralph.

"No kidding," said Frank. "Where are you headed now?"

"I don't know exactly," said Ralph. "Where are *you* going?"

"To the woods—want to come along?" said Frank.

"Sure," said Ralph. "What's the woods?"

"Oh, it's cool," said Frank. "Big trees, wild stuff, plants with berries—the whole thing. No people, and lots of animals. A nice crowd."

"Sounds good," said Ralph. "Which way?"

"Just keep pedaling," said Frank.

After a couple of hours, they had left the last town far behind, and the sun was coming out. Ralph was getting tired, but Frank kept saying, "Straight ahead, we're almost there!"

"This is it," said Frank when they came to the woods at last. "What do you think?"

"It looks okay," said Ralph.

"Let's go," said Frank.

The Woods

Ralph and Frank walked into the woods, and it was beautiful, but Ralph didn't see any animals. "Where is everybody?" he asked.

"Oh, they're around," said Frank. He knocked on a hollow tree.

"Yes?" said a voice.

"Stick your head out and say hello to my pal Ralph," called Frank.

A moment later, a raccoon peered out. "How do you do?" he said.

"Hi," said Ralph.

"Ralph's going to be with us for a while," said Frank.

"Splendid," said the raccoon.

Then Frank introduced Ralph to a deer who was standing nearby. Ralph had not even noticed the deer, because she stood so quietly.

Frank and Ralph walked farther into the woods.

"These are the opossums, directly overhead," said Frank.

"Hello," said Ralph.

"Welcome to the woods," said the opossums.

"Don't step on the turtle," said Frank.

"How do you do?" said Ralph.

"Pleased to meet you," said the turtle.

27

Pretty soon, Ralph was saying hello to all sorts of animals—a skunk, a chipmunk, an owl, a beaver, a frog. Everyone was friendly.

Then Frank introduced Ralph to two bears. "Meet Herb and Paul," he said.

"Hi," said Ralph.

"It's always good to see a new bear," said Herb.

"Welcome," said Paul.

A lot of the animals gathered around and asked Ralph to tell them about the circus. Ralph told all about the acrobats and the clowns and the elephants and the band and the popcorn and the roustabouts and the train.

Then the animals asked him to do his act, so Ralph showed how he rode his bike. All the animals said he was very good.

The next day Ralph and Frank played with the bears. Herb and Paul showed Ralph how to climb trees.

They showed him a good place to go swimming too. Ralph had a wonderful time.

One day in November, when the wind was blowing the last few leaves off the trees, Ralph hurried to play with Herb and Paul as usual.

"Hey," said Ralph. "What do you want to do today?"

"Nothing," said Herb. "We're all through for this year. We're going to hibernate now."

"Hibernate?" said Ralph.

"Sure," said Herb. "Don't *you* hibernate?"

"I don't know," said Ralph. "What is it?"

"We go to sleep for the winter," said Herb.

"You really sleep for the whole winter?" said Ralph.

"Bears always sleep for the winter," said Herb.

"Every year," said Paul. "Then, in the spring, we wake up and go out, and it's really great."

"Oh," said Ralph.

"You want us to show you a good cave to hibernate in?" asked Paul.

"No, thanks," said Ralph. "I couldn't possibly sleep all winter."

"Well, too bad, Ralph," said Herb. "There won't be much doing around here for the next few months. Just a lot of snow and ice and cold wind."

Ralph began to feel very lonely. "I guess I'll leave the woods," he said. "Go someplace else."

But Ralph knew there was no place else to go.

Ralph looked at his bike. A few snowflakes fell, and the air was cold. He walked around the woods, taking a last look at everything—the trees he had played in with Herb and Paul, the place where they swam.

Ralph was sitting against a tree when the skunk came along.

"Hey, Ralph," said the skunk. "You going to be sitting here for a minute?"

"I guess so," said Ralph.

"Good," said the skunk. "Don't move."

The skunk disappeared for a few minutes. Ralph could hear some of the animals talking. He heard Frank saying, "Quiet, everybody—quiet!"

And he heard the owl hoot. He couldn't figure out what was going on. Then the skunk came back.

The skunk climbed on a rock and said, "We have a surprise for you, Ralph. We are now going to present the Big Woods Circus!"

As Ralph watched, the beaver ran out and did a juggling act with acorns.

The possums swung from a tree branch while the frog, the woodpecker, and the owl made music.

Herb and Paul did a clown act, tripping and falling down a lot.

Frank did a balancing act with the turtle and the chipmunk.

The deer ran out with two raccoons on her back.

The squirrels did an act flying through the air, high up in the trees.

Afterward, all the animals came out and bowed. Ralph clapped and clapped.

"It was as good as the other circus," said Ralph. "Maybe even better."

Frank said, "We did the circus for you because we want you to stay in the woods with us. Everybody likes you, and we don't want you to leave. We want to do another circus next year with you as the star, showing us how. Then maybe we could put it on for the other animals over on Black Mountain."

"Will you stay?" asked the chipmunk.
"Will you?" said the skunk.
"How about it?" said Paul.
Ralph smiled. "Okay," he said.
Everybody cheered.

"I picked you out a cave, just in case," said Frank.
He took Ralph to a cave on the side of a hill.
"There it is," said Frank. "Nice and quiet."
Ralph went in and took a look around.

"Perfect place to hibernate," said Frank. "Very restful." Then he added, "I put your pajamas there, just in case..."

"Thanks, Frank," said Ralph. "I'll give it a try." He put on his pajamas.

Frank said he'd be back in a minute—he wanted to go get an acorn or two.

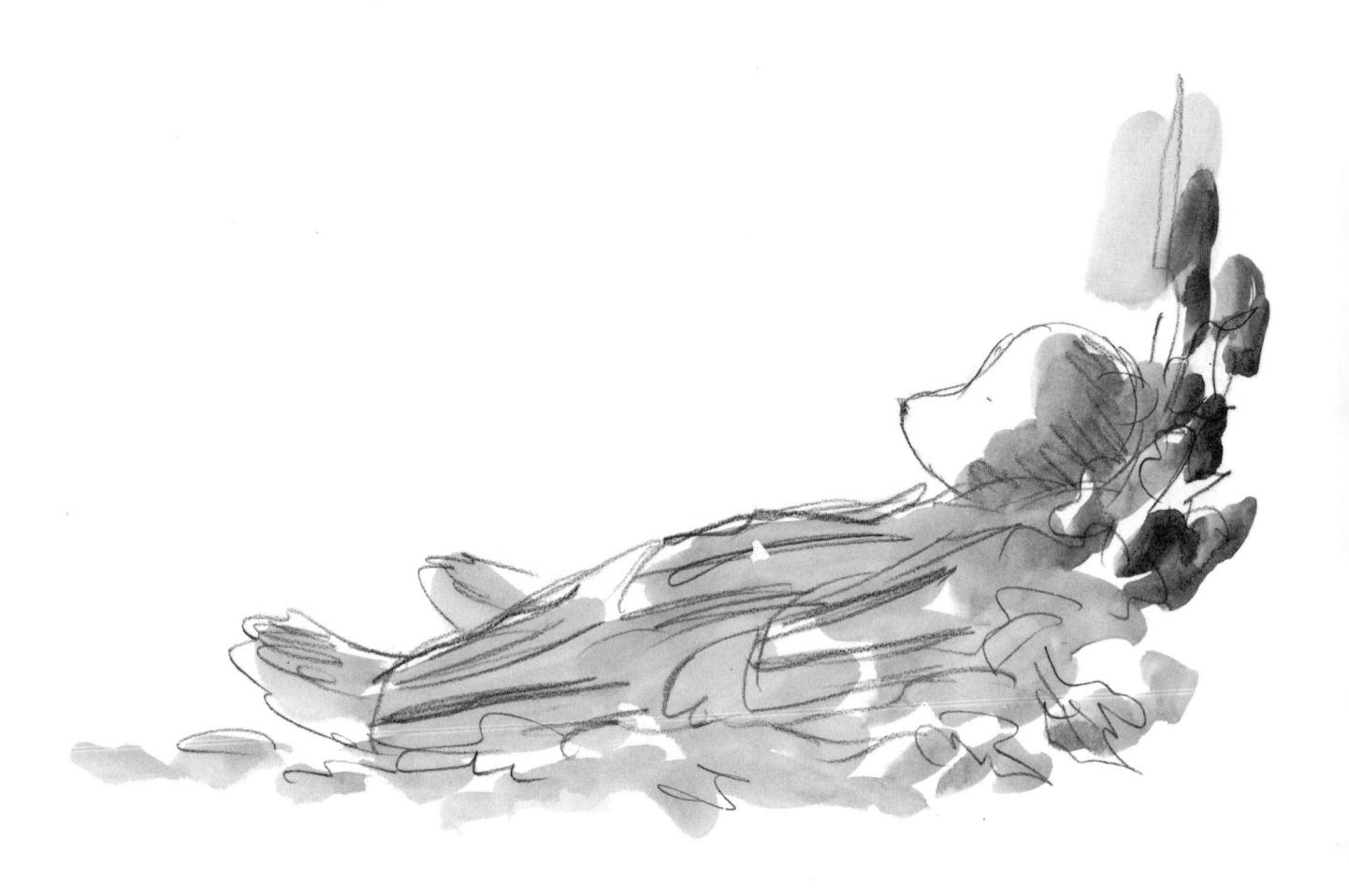

The leaves were really comfortable. Ralph thought about his new friends and his new life in the woods. He began to get sleepy. He imagined what it would be like in the spring.

By the time Frank got back a few minutes later, Ralph was sound asleep.

Ralph slept all winter long.

And when he finally woke up—

it was spring, and he could hear Herb and Paul and everybody already playing in the woods.

"Wait for me, everybody—I just woke up!" Ralph yelled. "Wait for me!"

And he ran, as fast as he could, to join them.

The
End